INVESTMENT
GUIDE
FOR
BEGINNERS

John Kennedy Akotia

ISBN-10:1512102369

Request for information should be addressed to
John Kennedy Akotia
Destiny Impact Publications
P. O. Box 299
Bolgatanga, UER, Ghana, W/A
Tel: +233-24 4451746/50 2538473
E-mail: fitzjkenny@yahoo.co.uk

Table of Contents

Introduction

Have you ever wondered how the rich got their wealth and then kept it growing? Do you dream of retiring early or of being able to retire at all? Do you know that you should invest, but don't know where to start?

If you answered "yes" to any of the above questions, then you are holding the right book at the right time. In this "Investment Guide for Beginners" book we will cover the practice of investing from the ground up. The world of finance can be extremely intimidating, but I firmly believe that the stock market and greater financial world won't seem so complicated once you learn some of the jargon and major concepts.

I should emphasize, however, that investing is not a get-rich-quick scheme. Taking control of your personal finances will take work, and, yes, there will be a learning curve. But the rewards will far outweigh the required effort. Contrary to popular belief, you do not have to let banks, bosses or investment professionals push your money in directions that you do not understand. After all, no one is in a better position than you are to know what is best for you and your money.

Regardless of your personality type, lifestyle or interests, this book will help you to understand what investing is, what it means and how time earns money through compounding. But it does not stop there. The book will also teach you about the building blocks of the investing world and the markets. It will give you some insight into techniques and strategies and help you think about which investing strategies suit you best. So do yourself a lifelong favour and keep reading. And lastly: remember there are no "stupid" questions. If after reading this book you still have unanswered questions, I would love to hear from you.

Chapter 1

Understanding The Concept
Of Investing

What Is Investing?

Generally speaking, every activity that is done today but which yields profit at a later date can be described as an investment. Investment involves postponing your consumption today in order to put your savings to work. Investment can also be described as the bridge between having savings or surplus cash and reaping returns from that surplus cash. In other words, investing has the potential to move the savings or surplus funds of one person or entity to another who needs or requires those funds.

Investing is the act of committing money or capital to an endeavour with the expectation of obtaining an additional income or profit

It is actually pretty simple: investing means putting your money to work for you. Essentially, it is a different way to think about how to make money. Growing up, most of us were taught that you can earn an income only by getting a job and working. And that is exactly what most of us do. There is one big problem with that assumption which is that if you want more money, you have to work more hours and most probably work harder too. However, there is a limit to how many hours a day we can work, not to mention the fact that having a bunch of money is no fun if we don't have the leisure time to enjoy it.

You cannot create a duplicate of yourself to

increase your working time; so instead, you need to send an extension of yourself which is your money to work for you. That way, while you are putting in hours for your employer, or even mowing your lawn, sleeping, reading the paper or socializing with friends, you can also be earning money elsewhere at the same time. Quite simply, making your money work for you maximizes your earning potential whether or not you receive a raise, decide to work overtime or look for a higher-paying job.

There are many different ways you can go about making an investment. This includes putting money into stocks, bonds, mutual funds, or real estate among many other things, or starting your own business. Sometimes people refer to these options as "investment vehicles," which is just another way of saying "a way to invest." Each of these vehicles has advantages and disadvantages, which we will discuss in a later chapter of this book. The point is that it doesn't matter which method you choose for investing your money, the goal is always to put your money to work so it earns you an additional profit. Even though this is a simple idea, it is the most important concept for you to understand.

What Investing Is *Not*

Investing is *not* gambling. Gambling is putting money at risk by betting on an uncertain outcome with the hope that you might win money. Part of the confusion between investing and gambling, however, may come from the way some people use investment vehicles. For example, it could be argued that buying a stock based on a "hot tip" you heard at your office is essentially the same as placing a bet at a casino.

True investing doesn't happen without some action on your part. A "real" investor does not simply throw his or her money at any random investment opportunity; he or she performs thorough analysis and commits capital only when there is a reasonable expectation of profit. Yes, there still is risk, and there are no guarantees, but investing is more than simply hoping good luck will be on your side.

Chapter 2

The Importance And Benefits Of Investing

Investing is a necessary condition for creating wealth because it helps in the realization of your dreams such as buying a car, house, or paying for your child's education at a future date. Investing puts your savings to work to earn returns. It is impossible to create wealth without investing and to have a secured financial future that can afford you a comfortable retirement.

Obviously, everybody wants more money and it is pretty easy to understand that people invest because they want to increase their personal financial freedom, the sense of security and ability to afford the things they want in life. However, in recent times, investing is becoming more of a necessity.

The days when everyone worked the same job for 30 to 35 years and then retired to a nice fat pension are gone as governments world around are tightening their economic belts. Almost without exception, the responsibility of planning for retirement is shifting away from the state and towards the individual. There is much debate over how safe our old-age pension programs will be over the next 20, 30 and 50 years. But why leave it to chance? By planning ahead you can ensure financial stability during your retirement. Investing is very important because it is a time-honoured practice for increasing your wealth.

There are several benefits to be derived from investing. The obvious benefit is the profits that accrue on an investment. For instance, when you invest in shares listed on any Stock Exchange, you can earn dividends or capital gains or both. Dividends are the portion of a company's profits that are distributed to all shareholders during a particular financial year after they have been recommended by the directors and approved by shareholders. Capital gains on the other hand refer to the difference in the price at which an investor buys shares and the price at which he sells them.

Another benefit of investing is that you protect your savings from the effects of inflation which can erode the value of your savings if not invested properly. The concept of the Time Value of money suggests that an amount of money you own today may not have the same value as in purchasing power tomorrow. For example, a one thousand dollars (\$ 1, 000.00) in 2015 will buy less goods in 2017 than would have been possible in 2015.

Another benefit of Investing is that it also helps you to prepare for projects in the future as well as retirement. Though you may not have the resources today to pursue your dream items such as acquiring immovable/movable assets (land, building, car etc.), regular investment can prepare you to realize these dreams in the future. Do not forget that a farmer can rather choose to consume his seed today or invest it in the soil to reap a harvest tomorrow. Choose to invest today for a better tomorrow.

Chapter 3

Basic Investment Objectives

An investment is made because it serves some objective for an investor. And depending on a person's current age, stage or position in life, risk appetite of the investor and personal circumstances, there are three main objectives or factors that influence an investment decision. These are safety of capital, earning current income and capital appreciation or growth.

While every investor invests with a specific objective in mind, and each investment has its own unique set of benefits and risks, it is possible for an investor to have more than one of these objectives. However, it is worth noting that the success of one must come at the expense of others.

For example, a 75-year old widow living off of her retirement portfolio would be far more interested in preserving the value of her investments than a 30-year-old business executive would be. Because the widow needs income from her investments to survive, she cannot risk losing her investment. The young executive, on the other hand, has time on his or her side. As investment income is not currently paying the bills, the executive can afford to be more aggressive in his or her investing strategies.

An investor's financial position will also affect his or her objectives. A multi-millionaire is obviously going to have much different goals than a newly married couple just starting out. For example, the millionaire, in an effort to increase his profit for the year, might have no problem putting down $ 100,000 in a speculative real estate investment. To him, the said amount is only a small percentage of his overall worth. The newly married couple however, may be concentrating on saving up for a down payment on a house and cannot afford to risk losing their money in a speculative venture. Regardless of the potential returns of a risky investment, speculation is just not appropriate for the young couple.

As a general rule of investing, the shorter your investing time horizon, the more conservative you should be and longer your investing time horizon, the more aggressive you should be. For instance, if you are investing primarily for retirement and you are still in your 20s, you still have plenty of time to make up for any losses you might incur along the way. At the same time, if you start when you are young, you don't have to put huge chunks of your pay cheque away every month because you have the power of compounding on your side.

On the other hand, if you are about to retire, it is very important that you either safeguard or increase the money you have accumulated. Because you will soon need to be accessing your investments, you don't want to expose all of your money to volatility - you don't want to risk losing your investment money in a market slump right before you need to start accessing your assets.

In this chapter therefore, we want to examine these three types of objectives, and the investment products that are used to achieve them and the ways in which investors can incorporate them in devising an investment strategy.

Safety

While no investment option is completely safe, there are products that are preferred by investors who are risk averse. Some individuals invest with an objective of keeping their money safe, irrespective of the rate of return they receive on their capital. Such near-safe products include fixed deposits, savings accounts, government bonds, etc.

We can get close to ultimate safety for our investment funds through the purchase of government-issued securities in stable economic systems, or through the purchase of the highest quality corporate bonds issued by the economy's top companies. Such securities are arguably the best means of preserving principal while receiving a specified rate of return.

The safest investments however, are usually found in the money market, which includes such securities as Treasury bills (T-bills), certificates of deposit (CD), commercial paper or bankers' acceptance slips, or in the fixed income (bond) market in the form of municipal and other government bonds, and in corporate bonds. The securities listed above are ordered according to the typical spectrum of increasing risk and, in turn, increasing potential yield. To compensate for their higher risk, corporate bonds return a greater yield than T-bills.

It is important to realize that there is an enormous range of relative risk within the bond market. At one end are government and high-grade corporate bonds, which are considered some of the safest investments around; at the other end are junk bonds, which have a lower investment grade and may have more risk than some of the more speculative stocks. In other words, it's incorrect to think that corporate bonds are always safe, but most instruments from the money market can be considered very safe.

Growth

While safety is an important objective for many investors, a majority of them invest to receive capital gains, which means that they want the invested amount to grow. There are several options in the market that offer this benefit. These include stocks, mutual funds, gold, property, commodities, etc. It is important to note that capital gains attract taxes, the percentage of which varies according to the number of years of investment.

Capital gains are entirely different from yield in that they are only realized when the security is sold for a price that is higher than the price at which it was originally purchased. Selling at a lower price is referred to as a capital loss. Therefore, investors seeking capital gains are likely not those who need a fixed, ongoing source of investment returns from their portfolio, but rather those who seek the possibility of longer-term growth.

Growth of capital is most closely associated with the purchase of common stock, particularly growth securities, which offer low yields but considerable opportunity for increase in value. For this reason, common stock generally ranks among the most speculative of investments as their return depends on what will happen in an unpredictable future. Blue-chip stocks *(Stock of a large, well-established and financially sound company that has operated for many years),* by contrast, can potentially offer the best of all worlds by possessing reasonable safety, modest income and potential for growth in capital generated by long-term increases in corporate revenues and earnings as the company matures. Yet rarely is any common stock able to provide the near-absolute safety and income-generation of government bonds.

It is also important to note that capital gains

offer potential tax advantages by virtue of their lower tax rate in most jurisdictions. Funds that are garnered through common stock offerings, for example, are often geared toward the growth plans of small companies, a process that is extremely important for the growth of the overall economy. In order to encourage investments in these areas, governments choose to tax capital gains at a lower rate than income. Such systems serve to encourage entrepreneurship and the founding of new businesses that help the economy grow.

Income

Some individuals invest with the objective of generating a second source of income. Consequently, they invest in products that offer returns regularly like bank fixed deposits, corporate and government bonds, etc.

The safest investments are also the ones that are likely to have the lowest rate of income return or yield. Investors must inevitably sacrifice a degree of safety if they want to increase their yields. This is the inverse relationship between safety and yield: as yield increases, safety generally goes down and vice versa.

In order to increase their rate of investment return and take on risk above that of money market instruments or government bonds, investors may choose to purchase corporate bonds or preferred shares with lower investment ratings. Investment grade bonds rated at A or AA are slightly riskier than AAA bonds, but presumably also offer a higher income return than AAA bonds. Similarly, BBB rated bonds can be thought to carry medium risk but offer less potential income than junk bonds, which offer the highest potential bond yields available but at the highest possible risk. Junk bonds are the most likely to default.

Most investors, even the most conservative-minded ones, want some level of income generation in their portfolios, even if it is just to keep up with the economy's rate of inflation. But maximizing income return can be an irresistibly strong principle for a portfolio, especially for individuals who require a fixed sum from their portfolio every month. A retired person who requires a certain amount of money every month is well served by holding reasonably safe assets that provide funds over and above other income-generating assets, such as pension plans, for example.

Other objectives

While the aforementioned objectives are the most common ones among investors today, some other objectives which may be described as secondary include:

Tax exemption

Some people invest their money in various financial products solely for reducing their tax liability. Some products offer tax exemptions while many offer tax benefits on long-term profits. A highly-paid executive, for example, may want to seek investments with favourable tax treatment in order to lessen his or her overall income tax burden. Making contributions to tax-sheltered retirement plan can be an effective tax minimization strategy.

Liquidity/Marketability

Many investment options are not liquid. This means they cannot be sold and converted into cash instantly. However, some people prefer investing in options that can be used during emergencies. Such liquid instruments include stock, money market instruments and exchange-traded funds, to name a few.

Common stock is often considered the most liquid of investments, since it can usually be sold within a day or two of the decision to sell. Bonds can also be fairly marketable, but some bonds are highly illiquid, or non-tradable, possessing a fixed term. Similarly, money market instruments may only be redeemable at the precise date at which the fixed term ends. If an investor seeks liquidity, money market assets and non-tradable bonds aren't likely to be held in his or her portfolio.

The Bottom Line

As we have seen from each of the five objectives discussed above, the advantage of one often comes at the expense of the benefits of another. If an investor desires growth, for instance, he or she must often sacrifice some income and safety. Therefore, most portfolios will be guided by one pre-eminent objective, with all other potential objectives occupying less significant weight in the overall scheme.

Choosing a single strategic objective and assigning weightings to all other possible objectives is a process that depends on such factors as the investor's temperament, his or her stage of life, marital status, family situation and so forth. Out of the multitude of possibilities out there, each investor is sure to find an appropriate mix of investment opportunities. You need only be concerned with spending the appropriate amount of time and effort in finding, studying and deciding on the opportunities that match your objectives.

Chapter 4

The Concept Of Compounding

Albert Einstein called compound interest **"the greatest mathematical discovery of all time"**. I think this is true, partly because, unlike the trigonometry or calculus you studied back in high school, compounding can be applied to everyday life.

The wonder of compounding, sometimes called "compound interest" transforms your working money into a state-of-the-art, highly powerful income-generating tool.

Compounding is the process of generating earnings on an asset's reinvested earnings. To work, it requires two things: the re-investment of earnings and time. The more time you give your investments, the more you are able to accelerate the income potential of your original investment, which takes the pressure off of you.

To demonstrate how compounding works, let us look at an example:

If you invest $10,000 today at 6%, you will have $10,600 in one year ($10,000 x 1.06). Now let us say that rather than withdraw the $600 gained as interest on your initial invested capital of $10,000, you keep it in there for another year. If you continue to earn the same rate of 6%, your investment will grow to $11,236.00 ($10,600 x 1.06) by the end of the second year.

Because you reinvested that $600, it works together with the original investment, earning you $636, which is $36 more than the previous year's interest earning of $600. This little bit of extra interest earning may in the beginning seem like peanuts, but let us not forget that you did not have to lift a finger to earn that additional $36. More importantly, this $36 also has the capacity to earn interest. After the next year, your investment will be worth $11,910.16 ($11,236 x 1.06). This time you earned $674.16, which is $74.16 more interest than the first year. This increase in the amount made each year is compounding in action: interest earning interest on interest and so on. This will continue as long as you keep reinvesting and earning interest.

Starting Early

The greatest ally to compounding is time. The more of time an investor has on his side the better the reward of compounding to that investor. Consider two individual investors, we will name them Suzann and Bob. Both Suzann and Bob are the same age. When Suzann was 25 she invested $15,000 at an interest rate of 5.5%. For simplicity, let us assume the interest rate was compounded annually. By the time Suzann reaches 50, she will have $57,200.89 that is ($15,000 x [1.055^25]) in her bank account.

Suzann's friend, Bob, did not start investing until he reached age 35. At that time, he invested $15,000 at the same interest rate of 5.5% compounded annually. By the time Bob reaches age 50, he will have $33,487.15 that is ($15,000 x [1.055^15]) in his bank account.

What happened? Both Suzann and Bob are 50 years old, but Suzann has $23,713.74 which is ($57,200.89 - $33,487.15) more in her savings account than Bob, even though Bob too invested the same amount of money. By giving her investment more time to grow, Suzann earned a total of $42,200.89 in interest whereas Bob earned only $18,487.15.

When you invest, always keep in mind that compounding amplifies the growth of your working money. Just like investing maximizes your earning potential, compounding maximizes the earning potential of your investments - but remember, because time and reinvesting make compounding work, you must keep your hands off the principal and earned interest.

Chapter 5

Types Of Investments

We have already mentioned that there are many ways to invest your money. Of course, to decide which investment vehicles are suitable for you, you need to know their characteristics and why they may be suitable for a particular investing objective.

Bonds

Grouped under the general category called fixed-income securities, the term bond is commonly used to refer to any securities that are founded on debt. When you purchase a bond, you are lending out your money to a company or government. In return, they agree to give you interest on your money and eventually pay you back the amount you lent out.

The main attraction of bonds is their relative safety. If you are buying bonds from a stable government, your investment is virtually guaranteed, or risk-free. The safety and stability, however, come at a cost. Because there is little risk, there is little potential return. As a result, the rate of return on bonds is generally lower than other securities.

Stocks

When you purchase stocks, or equities, as your advisor might put it, you become a part owner of the business. This entitles you to vote at the shareholders' meeting and allows you to receive any profits that the company allocates to its owners. These profits are referred to as dividends.

While bonds provide a steady stream of income, stocks are volatile. That is, they fluctuate in value on a daily basis. When you buy a stock, you are not guaranteed anything. Many stocks do not even pay dividends, in which case, the only way that you can make money is if the stock increases in value - which might not happen as well.

Compared to bonds, stocks provide relatively high potential returns. Of course, there is a price for this potential: you must assume the risk of losing some or all of your investment.

Mutual Funds

A mutual fund is a collection of stocks and bonds. When you buy a mutual fund, you are pooling your money with a number of other investors, which enables you (as part of a group) to pay a professional manager to select specific securities for you. Mutual funds are all set up with a specific strategy in mind, and their distinct focus can be nearly anything: large stocks, small stocks, bonds from governments, bonds from companies, stocks and bonds, stocks in certain industries, stocks in certain countries, etc.

The primary advantage of a mutual fund is that you can invest your money without the time or the experience that are often needed to choose a sound investment. Theoretically, you should get a better return by giving your money to a professional than you would if you were to choose investments yourself. In reality, there are some aspects about mutual funds that you should be aware of before choosing them, but we won't discuss them here.

Alternative Investments: Options, Futures, FOREX, Gold, Real Estate, Etc.

You now know about the two basic securities: equity and debt, better known as stocks and bonds. While many (if not most) investments fall into one of these two categories, there are numerous alternative vehicles, which represent the most complicated types of securities and investing strategies.

The good news is that you probably don't need to worry about alternative investments at the start of your investing career. They are generally high-risk/high-reward securities that are much more speculative than plain old stocks and bonds. Yes, there is the opportunity for big profits, but they require some specialized knowledge. So if you do not know what you are doing, you could get yourself into a lot of trouble. Experts and professionals generally agree that new investors should focus on building a financial foundation before speculating.

Chapter 6

Understanding The Money Market

What Is the Money Market?

The money market is a segment of the financial market in which financial instruments with high liquidity and very short maturities are traded. The money market is used by participants as a means for borrowing and lending in the short term, from several days to just under a year. Money market securities consist of negotiable certificates of deposit (CDs), banker's acceptances, Treasury bills, commercial paper, etc. Money market investments are also called cash investments because of their short maturities.

The money market is used by a wide array of participants, from a company raising money by selling commercial paper into the market to an investor purchasing CDs as a safe place to park money in the short term. The money market is typically seen as a safe place to put money due to the highly liquid nature of the securities and short maturities. Because they are extremely conservative, money market securities offer significantly lower returns than most other securities. However, there are risks in the money market that any investor needs to be aware of, including the risk of default on securities such as commercial paper.

Money market securities are essentially IOUs issued by governments, financial institutions and large corporations. These instruments are very liquid *(meaning they can quickly and easily be converted into cash)* and considered extraordinarily safe. Because they are extremely conservative, money market securities offer significantly lower returns than most other securities.

One of the main differences between the money market and the stock market is that most money market securities trade in very high denominations. This limits access for the individual investor. Furthermore, the money market is a dealer market, which means that firms buy and sell securities in their own accounts, at their own risk. Compare this to the stock market where a broker receives commission to acts as an agent, while the investor takes the risk of holding the stock. Another characteristic of a dealer market is the lack of a central trading floor or exchange. Deals are transacted over the phone or through electronic systems.

The easiest way for us to gain access to the

money market is with through money market mutual funds, or sometimes through a money market bank account. These accounts and funds pool together the assets of thousands of investors in order to buy the money market securities on their behalf. However, some money market instruments, like Treasury bills, may be purchased directly. Notwithstanding that, they can be acquired through other large financial institutions with direct access to these **markets**.

There are several different instruments in the money market which offer different returns and different risks. We will consider three major money market instruments, namely: Certificates of Deposit (CDs), Treasury Bills and Commercial Paper, which in my opinion are the most popularly used ones.

Treasury Bills (T-Bills)

T-bills are short-term government securities

that mature in one year or less from their issue date and are considered to be one of the safest investments though they do not provide a great return.

Treasury Bills (T-bills) are thought to be the most marketable **money** market security. Their popularity is mainly due to their simplicity. Essentially, T-bills are a way for the government to raise money from the public. As defined above, T-bills are short-term securities that **mature** in one year or less from their issue date. They are issued with three-month, six-month and one-year maturities. T-bills are purchased for a price that is less than their par (face) value; when they mature, the government pays the holder the full par value. Effectively, your interest is the difference between the purchase price of the security and what you get at maturity. For example, if you bought a 91-day T-bill at $9,800 and held it until maturity, you would earn $200 on your investment. This differs from coupon bonds, which pay interest semi-annually.

Treasury bills (as well as notes and bonds) are issued through a competitive bidding process at **auctions**. If you want to buy a T-bill, you submit a bid that is prepared either non-competitively or competitively. In non-competitive bidding, you will receive the full amount of the security you want at the return determined at the auction. With competitive bidding, you have to specify the return that you would like to receive. If the return you specify is too high, you might not receive any securities, or just a portion of what you bid for.

The biggest reason for which T-Bills are so popular is that they are one of the few money market instruments that are affordable to the individual investors. T-bills are usually issued in denominations of $1,000, $5,000, $10,000, $25,000, $50,000, $100,000 and $1 million. Other positives are that T-bills are considered to be the safest investments in the world because the government backs them. As a matter of fact, they are considered risk-free.

The only disadvantage to T-bills is that you will not get a great return because Treasuries are exceptionally safe. Corporate bonds, certificates of deposit and money market funds will often give higher rates of interest. What is more is that, you might not get back all of your investment if you cash out before the maturity date.

Certificate Of Deposit (CD)

A certificate of deposit (CD) is a time deposit with a bank. CDs are generally issued by commercial banks but they can be bought through **brokerages**. They bear a specific maturity date (from three months to five years), a specified interest rate, and can be issued in any denomination, much like bonds. Like all time deposits, the funds may not be withdrawn on demand like those in a checking account.

CDs offer a slightly higher yield than T-Bills because of the slightly higher default risk for a bank but, overall, the likelihood that a large bank will go broke is pretty slim. Of course, the amount of interest you earn depends on a number of other factors such as the current interest rate environment, how much **money** you invest, the length of time and the particular bank you choose. While nearly every bank offers CDs, the rates are rarely competitive, so it is important to shop around before you settle for one.

A fundamental concept to understand when buying a CD is the difference between annual percentage yield (APY) and annual percentage rate (APR). APY is the total amount of interest you earn in one year, taking compound interest into account. APR is simply the stated interest you earn in one year, without taking compounding into account.

The difference results from when interest is paid. The more frequently interest is calculated, the greater the yield will be. When an investment pays interest annually, its rate and yield are the same. But when interest is paid more frequently, the yield gets higher. For example, say you purchase a one-year, $1,000 CD that pays 5% semi-annually. After six months, you'll receive an interest **payment** of $25 that is ($1,000 x 5 % x 0.5 years). Here is where the magic of compounding starts. The $25 payment starts earning interest of its own, which over the next six months amounts to $ 0.625 ($25 x 5% x 0.5 years). As a result, the rate on the CD is 5%, but its yield is 5.06. It may not sound like a lot, but compounding adds up over time.

The main advantage of CDs is their relative safety and the ability to know your return ahead of time. You will generally earn more than in a savings account, and you will not be at the mercy of the stock market.

Despite the benefits, there are two main disadvantages to CDs. First of all, the returns are quite small compared to many other investments. Furthermore, your money is tied up for the length of the CD and you will not be able to get it out without paying a harsh penalty.

Commercial Paper

For many corporations, borrowing short-term **money** from banks is often a laborious and annoying task. The desire to avoid banks as much as possible has led to the widespread popularity of commercial paper.

Commercial paper is an unsecured, short-**term loan** issued by a corporation, typically for financing accounts receivable and inventories. It is usually issued at a discount, reflecting current market interest rates. Maturities on commercial paper are usually no longer than nine months, with maturities of between one and two months being the average.

For the most part, commercial paper is a very **safe investment** because the financial situation of a company can easily be predicted over a few months. Furthermore, typically only companies with high credit ratings and credit worthiness issue commercial paper.

Commercial paper is usually issued in denominations of $100,000 or **more**. Therefore, smaller investors can only invest in commercial paper indirectly through money market funds like the Databank's M Fund.

Chapter 7

Understanding The Capital Market

Capital Markets

Capital markets the segment of financial markets designated for buying and selling medium to long term financial asserts such as equity and **debt** instruments. Capital markets channel savings and investment between suppliers of capital such as retail investors and institutional investors, and users of capital like businesses, government and individuals. Capital markets are vital to the functioning of an economy, since capital is a critical component for generating economic output. Capital markets include primary markets, where new stock and bond issues are sold to investors, and secondary markets, which trade existing securities.

Capital markets typically involve issuing instruments such as stocks and bonds for the medium-term and long-term. In this respect, capital markets are distinct from **money** markets, which refer to markets for financial instruments with maturities not exceeding one year.

Capital markets have numerous participants including individual investors, institutional investors such as **pension funds**, **mutual funds**, municipalities, governments, corporate organisations, banks and non-financial institutions. Suppliers of capital generally want the maximum possible return at the lowest possible risk, while users of capital want to raise capital at the lowest possible cost.

The size of a nation's capital markets is directly proportional to the size of its economy. The United States, the world's largest economy for example, has the biggest and deepest capital markets. Capital markets are increasingly interconnected in a globalized economy, which means that ripples in one corner can cause major waves elsewhere. The drawback of this interconnection is best illustrated by the global **credit** crisis of 2007-09, which was triggered by the collapse in U.S. mortgage-backed securities. The effects of this meltdown were globally transmitted by capital markets since banks and institutions in Europe and Asia held trillions of dollars of these securities.

In the capital markets, buyers or the investors buy the stocks or bonds of the sellers and trade them. If the seller, or issuer, is placing the securities on the market for the first time, then the market is known as the primary market. Conversely, if the securities have already been issued and are now being traded among buyers, this is done on the secondary market. Sellers make money off the sale in the primary market, not in the secondary market, although they do have a stake in the outcome (pricing) of their securities in the secondary market.

The buyers of securities in the capital market tend to use funds that are targeted for longer-term investment. Capital markets are risky markets and are not usually used to invest short-term funds. Many investors access the capital markets to save for retirement or education, as long as the investors have long time horizons, which usually means they are young and are risk takers.

There are both differences and similarities between capital and money markets. From the issuer or seller's standpoint, both markets provide a necessary business function: maintaining adequate levels of funding. The goal for which sellers access each market varies depending on their liquidity needs and time horizon. Similarly, investors or buyers have unique reasons for going to each market: Capital markets offer higher-risk investments, while money markets offer safer assets; money market returns are often low but steady, while capital markets offer higher returns. The magnitude of capital market returns is often a direct correlation to the level of risk; however, that is not always the case.

Although markets are deemed efficient in the long run, short-term inefficiencies allow investors to capitalize on anomalies and reap higher rewards that may be out of proportion to the level of risk. Those anomalies are exactly what investors in capital markets try to uncover. Although money markets are considered safe, they have occasionally experienced negative returns. Inadvertent risk, although unusual, highlights the risks inherent in investing - whether long or short term, money markets or capital markets.

Chapter 8

Types Of Investment Strategies

1. Aggressive Investment Strategy

An Aggressive Investment Strategy (AIS) is a portfolio management strategy that attempts to maximize returns by taking a relatively higher degree of risk. An aggressive investment strategy emphasizes capital appreciation as a primary investment objective, rather than income or safety of principal. Such a strategy would therefore have an **asset allocation** with a substantial weighting in stocks, and a much smaller allocation to fixed income and cash.

Aggressive **investment strategies** are especially suitable for young adults because their lengthy investment horizon enables them to ride out market fluctuations better than investors with a short investment horizon. Regardless of the investor's age, however, a high tolerance for risk is an absolute prerequisite for an aggressive investment strategy.

The aggressiveness of an investment strategy depends on the relative weight of high-reward, high-risk asset classes such as equities and commodities within the portfolio.

For example, Portfolio A which has an asset allocation of 75% equities, 15% fixed income and 10% commodities would be considered quite aggressive, since 85% of the portfolio is weighted to equities and commodities. However, it would still be less aggressive than Portfolio B, which has an asset allocation of 85% equities and 15% commodities.

But even within the equity component of an aggressive portfolio, the composition of stocks can have a significant **bearing** on its risk profile. For instance, if the equity component only comprises top-grade stocks, it would be considered less risky than if the portfolio only held small-capitalization stocks. If this is the case in the earlier example, Portfolio B could arguably be considered less aggressive than Portfolio A, even though it has 100% of its weight in aggressive assets.

An aggressive strategy needs **more** active management than a conservative "buy-and-hold" strategy, since it is likely to be much more volatile and would need more frequent adjustments to tailor it to changing market conditions. More frequent rebalancing would also be required to bring portfolio allocations back to their target levels, as the volatility of the assets that comprise an aggressive portfolio will quite often lead allocations to deviate significantly from the original or target weights.

2. Balanced/Hybrid Investment Strategy

A Balanced Investment Strategy (BIS) is a portfolio allocation and management method aimed at balancing risk and return. Such portfolios are generally divided equally between equities and fixed-income securities.

Although the balanced investment strategy aims to balance risk and return it does carry more risk than those strategies aiming at capital preservation or current income. This moderately aggressive portfolio is meant for individual investors with a longer time horizon (generally over five years) and that have an average risk tolerance. Investors who find these types of portfolios attractive are seeking to balance the amount of risk and return contained within the fund. This somehow hybrid portfolio would consist of approximately 50-55% equities, 35-40% bonds, 5-10% cash and equivalents.

3. Defensive Investment Strategy

A Defensive Investment Strategy (DIS) is a conservative method of portfolio allocation and management aimed at minimizing the risk of losing principal.

A defensive **investment strategy** entails regular portfolio rebalancing to maintain one's intended asset allocation; buying high-quality, short-maturity bonds and top-grade stocks; diversifying across both sectors and countries; placing stop loss orders; and holding cash and cash equivalents in down markets. Such strategies are meant to protect investors against significant losses from major market downturns.

The conservative or defensive investment

strategies, which put safety at a high priority, are most appropriate for investors who are risk averse and have a shorter time horizon. Conservative portfolios will generally consist mainly of cash and cash equivalents, or high-quality fixed-income instruments.

The main goal of a conservative or defensive portfolio strategy is to maintain the real value of the portfolio, or to protect the value of the portfolio against inflation. The portfolio you see here would yield a high amount of current income from the bonds and would also yield long-term capital growth potential from the investment in high quality equities.

With an offensive or aggressive investment strategy, in contrast, an investor tries to take advantage of a rising market by purchasing securities that are outperforming the market for a given level of risk and volatility. An offensive strategy may also entail **options**

trading and **margin trading**. Both offensive and defensive investment strategies require active management, so they may have higher investment fees and tax liabilities than a passively managed portfolio. A balanced investment strategy combines elements of both the defensive and offensive strategies.

Chapter 9

How To Choose Your Investment Types

Knowing Yourself

Investors can learn a lot from the famous Greek maxim inscribed on the Temple of Apollo's Oracle at Delphi: *"Know Thyself"*. In the context of investing, the wise words of the oracle emphasize that success depends on ensuring that your investment strategy fits your personal characteristics.

Even though all investors are trying to make

money, each one comes from a diverse background and has different needs. It follows that specific investing vehicles and methods are suitable for certain types of investors. Although there are many factors that determine which path is optimal for an investor, we will look at three main categories: investment objectives, investment time horizon and investing personality.

1. Investment Objectives

Generally speaking, investors have a few factors to consider when looking for the right place to park their money. Safety of capital, current income and capital appreciation are factors that should influence an investment decision and will depend on a person's age, stage or position in life and personal circumstances. For example an 55 year-old college teacher getting ready for retirement more likely to be interested in preserving the value of her investments than a 35 year-old business tycoon would be. Because the college teacher getting ready for retirement will soon need income from her investments to survive, he cannot risk losing his investment. The young business tycoon, on the other hand, has time on his side. As investment income is not currently paying his bills, he could afford to be more aggressive in his investing strategies.

An investor's financial position will also affect his or her objectives. A multi-millionaire is obviously going to have much different goals than a newly married couple just starting out in life. For example, the millionaire, in an effort to increase his profit for the year, might have no problem putting down $100,000 in a speculative real estate investment. To him, a hundred grand is a small percentage of his overall worth. Meanwhile, the couple is concentrating on saving up for a down payment on a house and cannot afford to risk losing their money in a speculative venture. Regardless of the potential returns of a risky investment, speculation is just not appropriate for the young couple.

2. Investment Time Horizon

Investment time horizon refers to the period of time an investor is prepared to wait for his investment to mature. The investment time horizon is determined by the investor. For instance, Mrs. Jones may have $10,000 today to invest and would want it back in four months while Mr. Kennedy who has the same amount to invest may need the money back in 5years. In this case Mrs. Jones has a short-term investment horizon while Mr. Kennedy has a long-term investment horizon. Investments products typically have different maturities from short term to long term so knowing your investment time horizon will help you to select the right investment.

As a general rule, the shorter your time horizon, the more conservative you should be. For instance, if you are investing primarily for retirement and you are still in your 30s, you still have plenty of time to make up for any losses you might incur along the way. At the same time, if you start when you are young, you don't have to put huge chunks of your pay cheque away every month because you have the power of compounding on your side.

On the other hand, if you are about to retire, it is very important that you either safeguard or increase the money you have accumulated. Because you will soon be accessing your investments, you don't want to expose all of your money to volatility - you don't want to risk losing your investment money in a market slump right before you need to start accessing your assets.

3. Investment Personality

What is your style? Do you love fast cars, extreme sports and the thrill of a risk? Or do you prefer reading in your hammock while enjoying the calmness, stability and safety of your backyard?

Peter Lynch, one of the greatest investors of all time, has said that the *"key organ for investing is the stomach, not the brain"*. In other words, you need to know how much volatility you can stand to see in your investments. Figuring this out for yourself is far from an exact science; but there is some truth to an old investing maxim: you have taken on too much risk when you can't sleep at night because you are worrying about your investments.

Another personality trait that will determine your investing path is your desire to research investments. Some people love nothing more than digging into financial statements and crunching numbers. To others, the terms balance sheet, income statement and stock analysis sound as exciting as watching paint dry. Others just might not have the time to go through prospectuses and financial statements.

What is Your Risk Tolerance Level?

By now it is probably clear to you that the main thing determining what works best for an investor is his or her capacity to take on risk. We have mentioned some core factors that determine risk tolerance, but remember that every individual's situation is different and that what we have mentioned is far from a comprehensive list of the ways in which investors differ from one another. The important point of this section is that an investment is not the same to all people. Now that you have a general idea of what investing is and why you should do it, it is time to learn about how investing lets you take advantage of one of the miracles of mathematics: compound interest.

Chapter 10

Investment Asset Allocation

With literally thousands of stocks, bonds and mutual funds to choose from, picking the right investments can confuse even the most seasoned investor. However, starting to build a portfolio with stock picking might be the wrong approach. Instead, you should start by deciding what mix of stocks, bonds and mutual funds you want to hold - this is referred to as your asset allocation.

What Is Asset Allocation?

Asset allocation is an investment portfolio technique that aims to balance risk and create diversification by dividing assets among major categories such as cash, bonds, stocks, real estate and derivatives. Each asset class has different levels of return and risk, so each will behave differently over time. For instance, while one asset category increases in value, another may be decreasing or not increasing as much. Some critics see this balance as a settlement for mediocrity, but for most investors it is the best protection against a major loss should things ever go wrong in one investment class or sub-class.

The consensus among most financial professionals is that asset allocation is one of the most important decisions that investors make. In other words, your selection of stocks or bonds is secondary to the way you allocate your assets to high and low-risk stocks, to short and long-term bonds, and to cash on the side-lines.

Five Things to Know About Asset Allocation

We must emphasize that there is no simple formula that can find the right asset allocation for every individual. We can, however, outline five points that are deemed important when thinking about asset allocation:

1. Risk vs. Return

The risk-return trade-off is at the core of what asset allocation is all about. It is easy for everyone to say that they want the highest possible return, but simply choosing the assets with the highest "potential" whether stocks or derivatives is not the answer. The crashes of 1929, 1981, 1987, and the more recent declines of 2007-2009 are all examples of times when investing in only stocks with the highest potential return was not the most prudent plan of action. It is time to face the truth: every year your returns are going to be beaten by another investor, mutual fund, pension plan, etc. What separates greedy and return-hungry investors from successful ones is the ability to weigh the difference between risk and return. Yes, investors with a higher risk tolerance should allocate more money into stocks. But if you cannot keep invested through the short-term fluctuations of a bear market, you should cut your exposure to equities.

2. Do Not Rely Solely on Financial Software or Planner Sheets

Financial planning software and survey sheets designed by financial advisors or investment firms can be beneficial, but never rely solely on software or some pre-determined plan. For example, one old rule of thumb that some advisors use to determine the proportion a person should allocate to stocks is to subtract the person's age from 100. In other words, if you are 35 year, you should put 65% of your money into stocks and the remaining 35% into bonds, real estate and cash.

But standard worksheets sometimes don't take into account other important information such as whether or not you are a parent, retiree or spouse. Other times, these worksheets are based on a set of simple questions that don't capture your financial goals. Remember, financial institutions love to peg you into a standard plan not because it's best for you, but because it's easy for them. Rules of thumb and planner sheets can give people a rough guideline, but don't get boxed into what they tell you.

3. Determine Your Long- and Short-Term Goals

We all have our goals. Whether you aspire to own a yacht or vacation home, to pay for your child's education or to simply save up for a new car, you should consider it in your asset allocation plan. All of these goals need to be considered when determining the right mix.

For example, if you're planning to own a retirement condo on the beach in 20 years, you need not worry about short-term fluctuations in the stock market. But if you have a child who will be entering college in five to six years, you may need to tilt your asset allocation to safer fixed-income investments.

4. Time Is Your Best Friend

The U.S. Department of Labour has said that for every 10 years you delay saving for retirement or some other long-term goal, you will have to save three times as much each month to catch up. Having time not only allows you to take advantage of compounding and the time value of money, it also means you can put more of your portfolio into higher risk/return investments, namely stocks.

5. Just Do It!

Once you have determined the right mix of stocks, bonds and other investments, it is time to implement it. The first step is to find out how your current portfolio breaks down. It is fairly straightforward to see the percentage of assets in stocks versus bonds, but do not forget to categorize what type of stocks you own (i.e. small, mid or large cap). You should also categorize your bonds according to their maturity (i.e. short, mid or long term). Mutual funds can be more problematic. Fund names do not always tell the entire story. You have to dig deeper in the prospectus to figure out where fund assets are invested.

The Bottom Line

There is no one standardized solution for allocating your assets. Individual investors require individual solutions. Furthermore, if a long-term horizon is something you do not have, don't worry. It is never too late to get started it is only too bad never starting. It is also never too late to give your existing portfolio a face-lift. Asset allocation is not a one-time event; it is a life-long process of progression and fine-tuning.

Chapter 11

Portfolios And Diversification

It is good to clarify how securities are different from each other, but it is even more important to understand how their different characteristics can work together to accomplish an objective.

The Portfolio

A portfolio is a combination of different investment assets mixed and matched for the purpose of achieving an investor's goals. Items that are considered a part of your portfolio can include any asset you own - from real items such as art and real estate, to equities, fixed-income instruments and their cash and equivalents. For the purpose of this beginners' guide to investing, we will focus on the most liquid asset types: equities, fixed-income securities, cash and equivalents.

An easy way to think of a portfolio is to imagine a pie chart, whose portions each represent a type of vehicle to which you have allocated a certain portion of your whole investment. The asset mix you choose according to your aims and strategy will determine the risk and expected return of your portfolio.

What Is Diversification?

Diversification in the most general sense can be summed up with this phrase: **"Don't put all of your eggs in one basket"**. While that sentiment certainly captures the essence of the issue, it provides little guidance on the practical implications of the role diversification plays in an investor's portfolio and offers no insight into how a diversified portfolio is actually created. In this section, we will provide an overview of diversification and give you some insight into how you can make it work to your advantage.

Taking a closer look at the concept of diversification, the idea is to create a portfolio that includes multiple investments in order to reduce risk. Consider, for example, an investment that consists of only stock issued by a single company. If that company's stock suffers a serious downturn, your portfolio will sustain the full impact of the decline. By splitting your investment between the stocks from two different companies, you can reduce the potential risk to your portfolio.

Another way to reduce the risk in your portfolio is to include bonds and cash. Because cash is generally used as a short-term reserve, most investors develop an asset allocation strategy for their portfolios based primarily on the use of stocks and bonds. It is never a bad idea to keep a portion of your invested assets in cash or short-term money-market securities. Cash can be used in case of an emergency, and short-term money-market securities can be liquidated instantly in case an investment opportunity arises, or in the event your usual cash requirements become critical and you need to sell investments to make payments. Also, keep in mind that asset allocation and diversification are closely linked concepts; a diversified portfolio is created through the process of asset allocation. When creating a portfolio that contains both stocks and bonds, aggressive investors may lean towards a mix of 80% stocks and 20% bonds, while conservative investors may prefer a 20% stocks to 80% bonds mix.

Regardless of whether you are aggressive or conservative, the use of asset allocation to reduce risk through the selection of a balance of stocks and bonds for your portfolio is a more detailed description of how a diversified portfolio is created rather than the simplistic eggs in one basket concept. With this in mind, you will notice that mutual fund portfolios composed of a mix, which includes both stocks and bonds, are referred to as "balanced" portfolios. The specific balance of stocks and bonds in a given portfolio is designed to create a specific risk-reward ratio that offers the opportunity to achieve a certain rate of return on your investment in exchange for your willingness to accept a certain amount of risk. In general, the more risk you are willing to take, the greater the potential return on your investment.

What Are My Options?
If you are a person of limited means or if you simply prefer uncomplicated investment scenarios, you could choose a single

balanced mutual fund and invest all of your assets in the fund. For most investors, this strategy is far too simplistic. While a given mix of investments may be appropriate for a child's college education fund, that mix may not be a good match for long-term goals, such as retirement or estate planning. Likewise, investors with large sums of money often require strategies designed to address more complex needs, such as minimizing capital gains taxes or generating reliable income streams. Furthermore, while investing in a single mutual fund provides diversification among the basic asset classes of stocks, bonds and cash (funds often hold a small amount of cash from which the fees are taken), the opportunities for diversification go far beyond these basic categories.

With stocks, investors can choose a specific style, such as focusing on large, mid or small caps. In each of these areas are stocks categorized as growth or value. Additional choices include domestic and foreign stocks. Foreign stocks also offer sub-categorizations that include both developed and emerging markets. Both foreign and domestic stocks are also available in specific sectors, such as biotechnology and healthcare.

In addition to the variety of equity investment choices, bonds also offer opportunities for diversification. Investors can choose long-term or short-term issues. They can also select high-yield or municipal bonds. Once again, risk tolerance and personal investment requirements will largely dictate investment selection.

While stocks and bonds represent the traditional tools for portfolio construction, a host of alternative investments provide the opportunity for further diversification. Real estate investment trusts, hedge funds, physical business and other investments provide the opportunity to invest in vehicles that do not necessarily move in tandem with the traditional financial markets. Yet these investments offer another method of portfolio diversification.

Concerns

With so many investments to choose from, it may seem like diversification is an easy objective to achieve, but that sentiment is only partially true. The need to make wise choices still applies to a diversified portfolio. Furthermore, it is possible to over-diversify your portfolio, which will negatively impact your returns. Many financial experts agree that 20 stocks is the optimal number for a diversified equity portfolio. With that in mind, buying 50 individual stocks or four large-cap mutual funds may do more harm than good. Having too many investments in your portfolio does not allow any of the investments to have much of an impact, and an over-diversified portfolio often begins to behave like an index fund. In the case of holding a few large-cap mutual funds, multiple funds bring the additional risks of overlapping holdings as well as a variety of expenses, such as low balance fees and varying expense ratios, which could have been avoided through a more careful fund selection.

Tools

Investors have many tools to choose from when creating a portfolio. For those lacking time, money or interest in investing, mutual funds provide a convenient option; there is a fund for nearly every taste, style and asset allocation strategy. For those with an interest in individual securities, there are stocks and bonds to meet every need.

The Bottom Line

Regardless of your means or method, keep in mind that there is no generic diversification model that will meet the needs of every investor. Your personal time horizon, risk tolerance, investment goals, financial means and level of investment experience will play a large role in dictating your investment mix. Start by figuring out the mix of stocks, bonds and cash that will be required to meet your needs. From there, determine exactly which investments to use in completing the mix, substituting traditional assets for alternatives as needed. If you are too overwhelmed by the choices or simply prefer to delegate, there are plenty of financial services professionals available to assist you.

Chapter 12

Investing On The Ghana Stock Exchange

Who Qualifies to Invest on the Ghana Stock Exchange?

If you are 18 years and above and of a sound mind you are qualified to invest on the Ghana Stock Exchange. You must also understand that investment on the Ghana Stock Exchange is long-term and that there are risks involved, especially during the short-term. Another qualification is to have an investment objective and a period of time in which you intend to retrieve your investment. Another requirement is that you must have some surplus funds you intend to investment. Parents can invest in trust for their children. Institutions can also invest their pension and provident funds on the Ghana Stock Exchange so long as the regulations governing those funds permit such investments.

How Much Can I Invest on the GSE?

The amount of money you need to invest on the Ghana Stock Exchange depends on the prices of shares you select. Shares are usually traded in batches or round lots of 100. Where the price of a particular stock is high, an investor can contact a broker to buy fewer than 100 shares or what is commonly referred to as odd lots.

How to the Select Stocks You Want to Invest in on the GSE?

A number of factors should be considered by an investor before selecting any security on the Ghana Stock Exchange. Sound investment is typically based on research. When you decide to invest in shares on the Ghana Stock Exchange, you must consider the past performance of companies, prevailing conditions in the sector in which the companies operate as well as the future outlook in terms of profit growth and dividend payment. An investor can obtain such research information either by contacting a stockbroker for advice and/or reading research reports produced by the stockbrokerage companies.

What Determines Share Prices?

Share prices are fundamentally determined by supply and demand. In stock market terminology, demand refers to bids and supply refers to offers. All other things remaining the same, the price of a share will go up if bids for the share exceed offers. Similarly, a share's price is most likely to fall if offers exceed bids for it. Bids and offers normally change in response to changing expectations of the investing public. Other factors behind demand and supply that affect share prices are interest rates, expectations of the market, the economy, performance of the listed company, major news from the listed company and investor psychology.

1. Interest Rate

Generally, interest rates and share price move in opposite directions. A fall in interest rates on money market instruments like Treasury bill, fixed deposits and call accounts make them less attractive in terms of the returns they yield. Investors typically react to such a fall by transferring their investments into the stock market. This can lead to an increase in demand for shares, which may trigger price increases. In the case of a rise in interest rates, the opposite occurs, all things being equal. Increases in lending rates can also have an indirect influence on share prices. Where the cost of loan capital of listed companies goes up with a rise in lending rates this could dampen net profits and hence share prices.

2. The Performance of the Economy

When an economy is prospering and doing well, the general level of income rises. This leads to an improvement in the disposable incomes of individuals. Demand for shares derives partly from the level of disposable income. All things being equal, the higher the ability of investors to buy shares, the higher the demand for shares and with it the tendency for share prices to move up. The opposite is also true as well. When an economy is sluggish, the level of income and hence disposable income is affected negatively. Such a situation may lead investors to cut back their investments in shares. The resulting slump in demand for shares could lead to a fall in share prices.

3. Investor Expectations

Expectations of the market have an impact on prices. Expectation of the market refers to what the investing public envisages the future performance of the stock market and listed companies to be. Specifically, the investing public will be interested in earnings growth and payment of dividend by the listed companies. Investors will typically buy shares of those companies that are expected to record strong growth rates in their earning and pay good dividends. The reason is that most investors are looking for profitable companies to invest in. This makes expectations about earnings growth and dividend payment key drivers of a company's share price.

4. Investor Psychology

There are some investors who buy when prices are generally going up and others who sell when prices are sliding. In most of these cases, the buying or selling behaviour of the investor is not influenced by fundamental operational performance. This behaviour sometimes described as "herd behaviour" is rooted in the psychology that if everybody is buying thus pushing the price up, there must be a good underlying reason and vice versa. This behaviour is a reflection of the survival instinct and the sheer number of investors who are influenced by it tilts the supply-demand equation in the market and hence prices. It is important to understand whether shares price are moving as a result of fundamentals or investors psychology (herd effect).

5. Company Announcement

Listed companies are expected to inform the general public about any significant development in their operations as well as their quarterly financial results. Listed companies therefore make announcements such as changes in their board of directors, key staff appointments and resignations, merger and acquisition moves, expansions of branch network/production floor, etc. The Ghana Stock Exchange also requires all listed companies to report their financial result quarterly. These company announcements either increase or reduce demand for shares.

Share Indexes

Indexes are widely used to track the direction of various stock markets. While the average indexes are calculated, all investors can benefit from the information given by these indexes. An index is an imaginary portfolio of securities representing a particular market or a portion of it. Each index has its own calculation methodology and is usually expressed in terms of a change from a base value. Thus, the percentage change is more important than the actual numeric value. Stock and bond market indexes are used to construct index mutual funds and exchange-traded funds

(ETFs) whose portfolios mirror the components of the index.

Indexes such as the GSE All-Share Index, Dow Jones, Nikkei and FTSE are examples of stock market indexes used in other markets. The Standard & Poor's 500 is one of the world's best known indexes, and is the most commonly used benchmark for the stock market.

In very simple terms, stock market indexes track changes in the market value of the stock exchange and thus show the performance of the stock market. The Ghana Stock Exchange currently has two official indexes referred to as the GSE Composite Index and the GSE Financial Stocks Index.

Monitoring Your Investments

An investment is not supposed to be done passively. It is important for an investor to actively follow or monitor his investment.

Monitoring your investment involves keeping your eye on the developments within the company you invested in, the stock market and the economy as a whole. It is a "hands on" affair. As an investors on the Ghana Stock Exchange, you can monitor their investments by keeping active communication lines with their broker, by reading the business pages of the newspapers, listening or watching business news on local FM stations and on the TV.

Why You Must Monitor Your Investments

The business world is dynamic as there is always one change or the other taking place. For instance, there could be a change in the environment of a company in which you hold shares. The change could affect the fortunes of the company either positively or negatively. If you are monitoring your investment, you will be in a better position to either take advantage of the opportunity or cut your losses. You can know the right time to shift your investment from one listed company to another or when to buy/sell an investment only when you monitor your investment.

Securing Your Investment on the Ghana Stock Exchange

Whenever you buy shares on the Ghana Stock Exchange, you are supposed to receive notification. The broker who executed your request is required to give you a contract note covering the transaction. Three days after the date of the transaction, your broker must settle the trade, that is you should receive cash if it was a sale or have your securities account credited with the number of shares purchased. Therefore it is necessary that as an investor on the Ghana Stock Exchange, you open a securities account with the GSE Securities through your broker.

Certain regulatory measures are in place to protect individuals who invest in securities on the Ghana Stock Exchange. The brokers who serve as intermediaries between investors and the Ghana Stock Exchange are required by the Ghana Stock Exchange to comply with membership regulations. The listed companies on the Ghana Stock Exchange are expected to observe certain rules including disclosure of result and any other information that are significant and price-sensitive. The Securities Industry Law regulates Ghana's capital market itself as well as all Dealers in the securities industry. Under this law, a Securities & Exchange Commission (SEC) has been established to ensure that all players in the industry comply with the standards established for operating in the industry. Investors must keep themselves informed and contact the Securities & Exchange Commission if they have any serious complaint.

How to Open a Securities Account

A prospective investor on the Ghana Stock

Exchange must open a securities account with a brokerage house prior to trading in securities. The process of opening an account is very simple and starts by making contact with a broker of your choice. The investor then completes an account opening form giving personal particulars, a passport picture and an identification such as Voter ID card, Driving licence, Passport, National ID card and contact address etc.

Trading Arrangement

Only Authorised Dealing Officers (brokers) can trade on the Ghana Stock Exchange. An Authorised Dealing Officer is a broker who has been licensed by the Ghana Stock Exchange to be a trader in securities. Trading on the Ghana Stock Exchange takes place every working day of the week from 10.00am to about 1.00pm. Trading is open to the general public.

A Stockbroker

A stockbroker is a professional who helps

investors to either buy or sell securities (shares and bonds). The stockbroker therefore acts as the middleman or intermediary between investors who wish to buy shares/bonds and those investors who wish to sell securities. The stockbroker therefore eliminates the need for investors to search for trading partners. The stockbroker also gives advice to investors about which securities to buy and sell. Stockbrokers play a vital role in our market because all investment on the Ghana Stock Exchange can only be done through a stockbroker. To qualify as a broker, a person must among other things complete the Securities Courses offered by the Ghana Stock Exchange, pass the relevant examinations in them, be in the employment of a brokerage company for at least six months and be licensed also by the Securities & Exchange Commission.

Listed Companies

Companies that have applied to the Ghana Stock Exchange and have been approved for their shares to be traded on the GSE are referred to as listed companies. These companies have complied with certain requirements of the Ghana Stock Exchange. All listed companies are public companies and they are all required to publicly disclose their results and other pertinent information affecting their operations. There are currently thirty seven (37) companies listed on the Ghana Stock Exchange representing some of the leading sectors in the Ghanaian economy. These sectors include financial, manufacturing, mining, trading, brewery and pharmaceuticals.

Chapter 13

Understanding Risk And Return Trade-Offs In Investment

You might be familiar with the risk-reward concept, which states that the higher the risk of a particular investment, the higher the possible return. But many investors do not understand how to determine the risk level their individual portfolios should bear. This chapter provides a general framework that any investor can use to assess his or her personal risk level and how this level relates to different investments.

Risk-Reward Concept

This is a general concept underlying anything by which a return can be expected. Anytime you invest money into something, there is a risk, whether large or small, that you might not get your money back. In turn, you expect a return, which compensates you for bearing this risk. In theory the higher the risk, the more you should receive for holding the investment and the lower the risk, the less you should receive.

For investment securities, we can create a chart with the different types of **securities** and their associated risk/reward profiles as seen in the diagram below.

Although this chart is by no means scientific, it provides a guideline that investors can use when picking different investments.

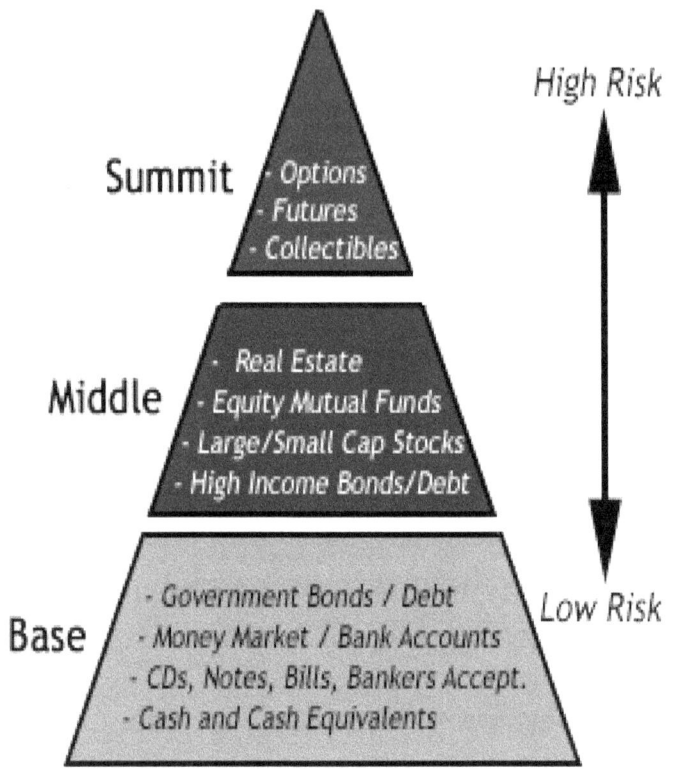

Located on the upper portion of this chart are investments that have higher risks but might offer investors a higher potential for above-average returns. On the lower portion are much safer investments, but these investments have a lower potential for high returns.

Determining Your Risk Preference

With so many different types of investments to choose from, how does an investor determine how much risk he or she can handle? Every individual is different, and it is hard to create a steadfast model applicable to everyone, but here are two important things you should consider when deciding how much risk to take:

Time Horizon

Before you make any investment, you should always determine the amount of time you have to keep your money invested. If you have $20,000 to invest today but need it in one year for a down payment on a new house, investing the money in higher-risk stocks is not the best strategy. The riskier an investment is, the greater its volatility or price fluctuations. So if your time horizon is relatively short, you may be forced to sell your securities at a significant loss.

With a longer time horizon, investors have more time to recoup any possible losses and are therefore theoretically more tolerant of higher risks. For example, if that $20,000 is meant for a lakeside cottage that you are planning to buy in 10 years, you can invest the money into higher-risk stocks. Why? Because there is more time available to recover any losses and less likelihood of being forced to sell out of the position too early.

Bankroll

Determination of the amount of money you can stand to lose is another important factor of figuring out your risk tolerance. This might not be the most optimistic method of investing; however, it is the most realistic. By investing only money that you can afford to lose or afford to have tied up for some period of time, you won't be pressured to sell off any investments because of panic or liquidity issues.

The more money you have, the more risk you are able to take. Compare, for instance, a person who has a net worth of $50,000 to another person who has a net worth of $5 million. If both invest $25,000 of their net worth into securities, the person with the lower net worth will be more affected by a decline than the person with the higher net worth. Furthermore, if the investors face a liquidity issue and require cash immediately, the first investor will have to sell off the investment while the second investor can use his or her other funds.

Investment Risk Pyramid

After deciding how much risk is acceptable in your portfolio by acknowledging your time horizon and bankroll, you can use the risk pyramid approach indicated in above for balancing your assets.

This pyramid can be thought of as an asset allocation tool that investors can use to diversify their portfolio investments according to the risk profile of each security. The pyramid, representing the investor's portfolio, has three distinct tiers:

a. *Base of the Pyramid* – The foundation of the pyramid represents the strongest portion, which supports everything above it. This area should consist of investments that are low in risk and have foreseeable returns. It is the largest area and comprises the bulk of your assets.

b. *Middle Portion* – This area should be made up of medium-risk investments that offer a stable return while still allowing for capital appreciation. Although more risky than the assets creating the base, these investments should still be relatively safe.

c. *Summit* – Reserved specifically for high-risk investments, this is the smallest area of the pyramid (portfolio) and should consist of money you can lose without any serious repercussions. Furthermore, money in the summit should be fairly disposable so that you don't have to sell prematurely in instances where there are capital losses.

Conclusion

Not all investors are created equally. While others prefer less risk, some investors prefer even more risk than others who have a larger net worth. This diversity leads to the beauty of the investment pyramid. Those who want more risk in their portfolios can increase the size of the summit by decreasing the other two sections, and those wanting less risk can increase the size of the base. The pyramid representing your portfolio should be customized to your risk preference.

It is important for investors to understand the idea of risk and how it applies to them. Making informed investment decisions entails not only researching individual securities but also understanding your own finances and risk profile. To get an estimate of the securities suitable for certain levels of risk tolerance and to maximize returns, investors should have an idea of how much time and money they have to invest and the returns they are seeking.

Chapter 14

Seven Investment Mistakes To Avoid

O f the mistakes made by investors, seven of them are repeat offenses. In fact, investors have been making these same mistakes since the dawn of modern markets, and will likely be repeating them for years to come. You can significantly boost your chances of investment success by becoming aware of these typical errors and taking steps to avoid them.

1. No Plan

As the old saying goes, if you don't know where you are going, any road will take you there. The solution is to have a personal investment plan or policy that addresses the following:

- *Goals and objectives* - Find out what you are trying to accomplish. Accumulating $100,000 for a child's college education or $2 million for retirement at age 60 are appropriate goals. Beating the market is not a goal.

- *Risks* - What risks are relevant to you or your portfolio? If you are a 30-year-old saving for retirement, volatility is not or should not be a meaningful risk. On the other hand, inflation which erodes any long-term portfolio is a significant risk.

- *Asset allocation* - What percentage of your total portfolio will you allocate to

GSE equities, international stocks, Government of Ghana bonds, high-yield bonds, etc. Your asset allocation should accomplish your goals while addressing relevant risks.

- *Diversification* - Allocating to different asset classes is the initial layer of diversification. You then need to diversify *within* each asset class. In GSE stocks, for example, this means exposure to large, medium and small cap stocks.

Your written plan's guidelines will help you adhere to a sound long-term policy, even when current market conditions are unsettling. Having a good plan and sticking to it is not nearly as exciting or as much fun as trying to time the markets, but it will likely be more profitable in the long term.

2. Too Short a Time Horizon

If you are saving for retirement 30 years hence, what the stock market does this year or next shouldn't be a big concern. Even if you are just entering retirement at age 70, your life expectancy is likely 15 to 20 years. If you expect to leave some assets to your heirs, then your time horizon is even longer. Of course, if you are saving for your daughter's college education and she is in junior high school, then your time horizon is appropriately short and your asset allocation should reflect that fact. Most investors are too focused on the short term.

3. Too Much Attention Given to Financial Media

There is almost nothing on financial news shows that can help you achieve your goals. Turn them off. There are few newsletters that can provide you with anything of value. Even if there were, how do you identify them in advance?

Think about it - if anyone really had profitable stock tips, trading advice or a secret formula to make big money, would they broadcast it on TV or sell it to you for $49 per month? No – they would keep their mouth shut, make their millions and not have to sell a newsletter to make a living. My advice to you therefore is to spend less time watching financial shows on TV and reading newsletters. Spend more time creating - and sticking to - your investment plan.

4. Not Rebalancing

Rebalancing is the process of returning your portfolio to its target asset allocation as outlined in your investment plan. Rebalancing is difficult because it forces you to sell the asset class that is performing well and buy more of your worst performing asset classes. This contrarian action is very difficult for many investors. In addition, rebalancing is unprofitable right up to that point where it pays off spectacularly and the underperforming assets start to take off. However, a portfolio allowed to drift with market returns guarantees that asset classes will be over-weighted at market peaks and underweighted at market lows a formula for poor performance.

5. Overconfidence in the Ability of Managers

From numerous studies on the returns from investing in equity mutual funds, we know that most managers will underperform their benchmarks. We also know that there is no consistent way to select in advance those managers that will outperform. We also know that very few individuals can profitably time the market over the long term. So why are so many investors confident of their abilities to time the market and select outperforming managers?

Investors' misplaced overconfidence in their ability to market-time and select outperforming managers leads directly to our next common investment mistake.

6. Not Enough Indexing

There is not enough time to cite many of the studies that prove that most managers and mutual funds underperform their benchmarks. Over the long-term, low-cost index funds are typically upper second-quartile performers, or better than 65-75% of actively managed funds.

Despite all the evidence in favour of indexing, the desire to invest with active managers remains strong. Indexing is sort of dull. You should try to index *(An index is a statistical measure of the changes in a portfolio of stocks representing a portion of the overall market.)* all or a large portion; say 70% to 80% of all your traditional asset classes. If you cannot resist the excitement of pursuing the next great performer, set aside a portion like 20% to 30% of each asset class to allocate to active managers. This may satisfy your desire to pursue outperformance without devastating your portfolio.

7. Chasing Performance

Many investors select asset classes, strategies, managers and funds based on recent strong performance. The feeling that "I am missing out on great returns" has probably led to more bad investment decisions than any other single factor. If a particular asset class, strategy or fund has done extremely well for three or four years, we know one thing with certainty: We should have invested three or four years ago. Now, however, the particular cycle that led to this great performance may be nearing its end. The smart money is moving out, and the dumb money is pouring in. Stick with your investment plan and rebalance, which is the polar opposite of chasing performance.

Conclusion

Investors who recognize and avoid these seven common mistakes give themselves a great advantage in meeting their investment goals. Most of the solutions above are not exciting. However, they are likely to be profitable and that is the ultimate reason why we really invest any way.

Other Titles by the Author

1. Turning Stumbling Blocks Into Stepping Stones
2. The Journey To Financial Freedom
3. Personal Career Decision Making
4. Exploits of Wisdom